PAINTING GREETING CARDS FOR FUN & PROFIT

Painting GREETING CARDS For FUN & PROFIT

Jeanette Robertson

NORTH LIGHT BOOKS

CINCINNATI, OHIO

DEDICATION

To my loving husband, Norman. Your smile lights my day.

Library of Congress Cataloging-in-Publication Data

Robertson, Jeanette
    Painting greeting cards for fun and profit / Jeanette Robertson.
        p.   cm.
    Includes index.
    ISBN 0-89134-907-3 (alk. paper)
    1. Greeting cards–Marketing. I. Title.
NC1860.R57 ·1999
741.6′84′0688–dc21   99-19203·
                                                      CIP

Editor: Joyce Dolan
Production editors: Christine Doyle and Marilyn Daiker
Production coordinator: Erin Boggs
Designer: Brian Roeth

ABOUT THE AUTHOR

PHOTO BY GENE GISSIN

For many years, Jeanette Robertson painted one-of-a-kind watercolors. Purchasers of her work would say, "This scene is so peaceful." Jeanette says, "I like it when a painting of mine touches a person in a positive way." But she wanted to "touch" more people than just with a few paintings here and there. "One of the lovely things about life is that you can choose to be surrounded by the beauty found in art."

So she began to submit her artwork to greeting card companies, which steadily bought her paintings. "I'm happy now that my 'peaceful' art touches more people. Cards are little expressions of art that everyone can afford to own."

Along with successfully selling her watercolors to card companies, she began her own small card company, Cottage Art. With so many talented artists living near her in central New York, she began teaching a course in designing and marketing greeting cards. This class helped other artists become part of the greeting card industry.

Robertson has a degree in textile design from the Fashion Institute of Technology in New York City. She has won numerous awards for her watercolors and silkscreen art.

Robertson lives in Cazenovia, New York, with her husband, Norman, and golden retriever, Casey.

ACKNOWLEDGMENTS

I give thanks to the many people and organizations who made this book possible. First to my mom and dad, Viola and (the late) George Acampara, for letting me be me. To the people working at the Cazenovia library for their help in finding reference books for me. To the Cazenovia College for making available the room where many students were able to learn about card design. To Joyce Dolan, my editor, who selflessly answered a lot of questions on weekends. To Dee DeRosa, who gave me inspiration to create when I first moved upstate. To art director Barbara Elliot—thank you. To Ellen Grossman for being a good friend when I needed it—many hugs to you. To the late Peggy Johnson, who gave me years of prayerful support while I pursued my art. To Janice Keefe and Gina Karl—two terrific art directors and ladies! To Joan Kantunis, whose Cape Cod "home" was the foundation of most of my art. To Anne Macleod—thanks to you, I have been designing cards for several years. To SUNY Morrisville—another card class that was a joy. To the Manlius library for finding information over the web. To North Light Books for giving many artists the opportunity to learn and create. To June Robertson—I am so grateful for your years of metaphysical support. To Glorial Rosenthal—your creative writing classes and friendship are treasures. To Phylis Smith, my lovely mother-in-law, for all of the hours you generously gave to being the second pair of eyes on the manuscript. To Syracuse University College for my very first students. To the Wellwood School in the Manlius and Fayetteville school system for the classroom I have used for a number of years. To Rachel Wolf, the editor who had the vision to see the need in the marketplace for this book. To Edith and Roy Walden, who gave me my first set of professional paints and brushes. And last but not least, many thanks to all my students and contributing artists.

Table of Contents

introduction

My cousin Michael and I used to take an annual trip to a quaint fishing village where the air is fresh and salty, and seagulls soar overhead. We always went shopping at a favorite store that specialized in nautical items. Every year I would stock up on note cards from Downcast Concepts, Inc. (formerly Cape Shore, Inc.), and make the same comment, "Gee, I could do this." Finally, after ten years, I found the courage to write to the company and enclosed photos of three of my paintings. A short time later, a letter arrived—they had bought two of my paintings!

Now that I've been freelancing for Downeast Concepts, Inc. for several years, I'm grateful to them for my beginnings. Since then I've learned what to do and what not to do. Having more knowledge about the design and business aspects of the industry, I have now sold to other companies, and started my own card company. Excited about designing cards, I also started teaching a course on it, and that successful course is now available to everyone through this book.

Can you imagine how exciting it is to see your art published for the first time on a card? It's a thrill! I enjoy knowing that my art can be shared with many people at an affordable cost. And it is even more exciting that every artist can have their art published in this form, whether through a publishing company or by self-publishing. This book will show you how.

With caring
thoughts
and loving
wishes.

ROSEMARY

CHAMOMILE

COMFREY

LAVE

nk You

chapter one

Get Started Making Cards

All you need to get started designing cards are some basic

art supplies. In this chapter I'll address a few of the most

popular mediums and other miscellaneous items that are

helpful. I'll also cover a few painting techniques I hope you'll

find fun to use on your cards.

Supplies

The following are materials I use to design my cards. Use this list as a suggestion to guide you when buying your own supplies.

Tube Paints

I use Winsor & Newton professional-quality watercolor paints in tubes. I squeeze out my tubes onto a John Pike palette. I also use Winsor & Newton gouache, an opaque watercolor. The watercolor colors I keep on hand are:

- Alizarin Crimson
- Antwerp Blue
- Burnt Sienna
- Burnt Umber
- Cadmium Red
- Cerulean Blue
- Cobalt Blue
- French Ultramarine
- Mauve
- New Gamboge
- Payne's Gray
- Prussian Blue
- Raw Umber
- Sap Green
- Sepia
- Winsor Green
- Winsor Red
- Winsor Yellow
- Yellow Ochre

Optional colors:
- Cadmium Yellow
- Opera (by Holbein)
- Permanent Rose
- Viridian

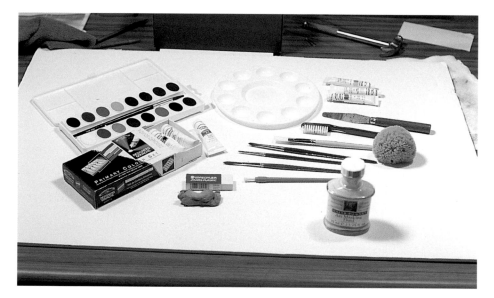

Art Supplies

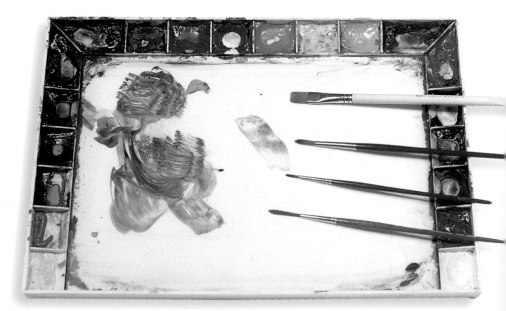

Palette With Tube Paint

Pan Paint

I also use pan paint, both transparent watercolors and gouaches, of which I own several different brands.

Liquid Watercolor

From time to time, I use liquid watercolor in bottles. They're available in sets or individually.

Gouache Tube Paint

Watercolor Tube Paint

Pan Paint

Bottled Watercolors

Colored Pencils

I use watercolor pencils by Derwent. I also have the waxy type of colored pencil, and I would recommend the Prismacolor brand. The pencils come in different-size sets or can be purchased individually. I treated myself to a box of 120.

Paper

I use Arches watercolor paper almost exclusively. Paper is one supply I don't skimp on! Use top-quality paper—it does make a difference in the finished work. I use 140 lb. (300gsm) cold-press most often.

When I'm using wax colored pencils, I prefer to work with either vellum or a regular finish surface drawing paper.

Watercolor Pencils

Wax Pencils

Brushes

I own some top-of-the-line Winsor & Newton Series 7 brushes, along with some much less expensive brands. I also use a few synthetic brushes that work well.

Basic to my collection are round brushes nos. 00, 1, 2, 4, 6 and 8, a rigger brush and a fan brush. I have two synthetic flat brushes—a 1-inch and a ½-inch.

Brushes

Miscellaneous Supplies

- liquid mask
- white eraser
- kneaded eraser
- kosher salt
- toothbrush
- knife
- razor
- ruling pen
- sea sponge
- rubber cement pickup
- throwaway brush
- pencils
- permanent markers
- masking tape

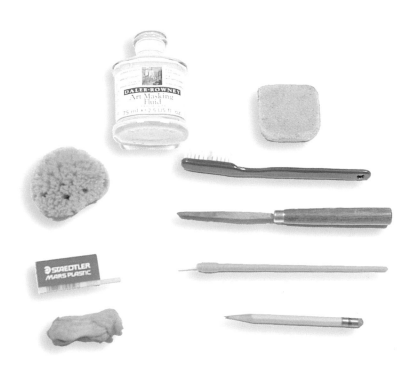

A few other supplies.

Techniques

Before we get into the chapters on greeting card art, here are a few illustrations on technique.

Splatter

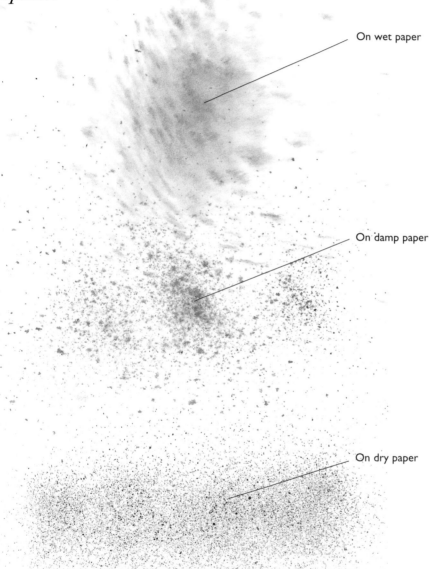

On wet paper

On damp paper

On dry paper

The splatter technique is great to use for sand, rocks, wood, brick and other textures. You'll need to use an old toothbrush and a knife. Put paint on the toothbrush and, while holding the loaded toothbrush over the knife, rub the brush forward over the knife. The amount of paint and how wet it is determines how the paint splatters onto the paper. The wetness of the paper also makes a difference in the finished product. When I use this technique, I make a few test "splatters" over scrap paper or newspaper until I get the consistency I want.

Kosher Salt

Kosher salt used on wet to damp paper is great for snowflakes or little puffs of wildflowers in a field. Use a pinch of salt in your fingers and sprinkle it on the desired areas. When it dries, it looks like tiny stars, snowflakes or flowers. Kosher salt can be found in most supermarkets.

Sea Sponge

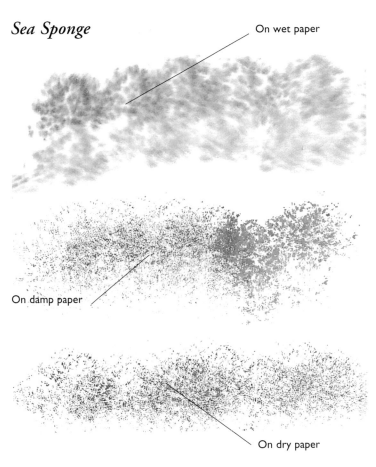

On wet paper

On damp paper

On dry paper

Sea Sponge

The texture created with a sea sponge is wonderful for depicting leaves, rocks and cliffs. Just dip the damp sponge into the paint and press it on your paper. First test it on scrap paper before you put it on your final design. A sea sponge has better texture than a man-made sponge. You can buy them in art supply stores or mail-order catalogs.

Pencil only

Pencil blended with water and brush

Watercolor Pencil

You can draw fine details with watercolor pencils, and you can leave texture where you want it. Blended with water, it's hard to tell the difference between the pencils and tube paints. You can combine the pencils with other mediums and just have fun experimenting with them.

Wax Pencil

Wax pencil—light drawing

Wax pencil—heavy drawing

Wax pencil—blended with colorless marker

Wax pencils are usually not used with other mediums. A card is created in its entirety with the pencils.

thank you

May your
special day
be filled with
love, laughter
and the magic
of life!

David Hughes

chapter two

Research and Approach Card Companies

Getting started selling greeting cards and note cards requires knowing how to find and contact a company to buy your cards. In this chapter we'll cover the three major ways to find appropriate companies for your cards and how to approach them with your designs. We'll also cover some technical aspects concerning submission of your art to card companies.

Finding Card Companies to Suit Your Style

Finding a company to freelance for is easy but requires research. The greeting card industry is a multibillion dollar business. Other than Hallmark, most companies buy their art from freelancers. Some artists sell a few designs here and there. Others develop a style, look or character that ends up being a licensed product for a company. Many artists have become famous over the years because of a collection of designs that the public raved over.

Before even thinking about research, you must determine what the style of your artwork is. Once you've figured out your style (you may have several), you need to find a company that's a good match for you.

Three ways to research a company to freelance for include visiting gift and card shops, reading trade publications and attending trade shows.

Gift and Card Shops

Visit several gift and card shops. Study the cards and consider the different companies that produce them. If you find one or more cards from a particular company that are similar to your style, send them a query letter or request their artist's guidelines. We'll talk more about the query letter and guidelines later.

LOUIE AWARDS

Louie Awards were started in the late 1980s. The awards were named in honor of Louis Prang, who brought the concept of greeting cards to the United States from Europe in the late 1880s. The awards are sponsored annually by the Greeting Card Association in Washington, DC, and given for many categories of greeting card design at the National Stationery Show in New York City.

SASE

When you request guidelines from a company, always include a self-addressed stamped envelope (SASE). Companies receive thousands of query letters every year. A SASE usually insures an answer and also shows that you are professional.

Louie Award Winner

©Renaissance Greeting Cards, Inc.
Created by Sherry Schmidt
B.D. Fox Supergroup

Trade Shows

There are many trade shows in small and large cities. The largest show is the National Stationery Show, which takes place every May at the Jacob Javits Center in New York City. There you'll find thousands of exhibitors. Many card companies send their art directors to these shows. This is a great place to research the card companies. You can get a good look at the different lines each one carries. You'll also find that some companies use a variety of styles and types of art.

Trade publications list all of the primary shows around the country. Shows are run differently with some charging an entrance fee, but most are open to the general public. Some shows allot special days for artists to show their work, but even if they don't, you may be able to arrange a quick interview if you have your portfolio with you. Realize, however, that you will make the most contacts and do the most business after the show. The card companies' primary goal at trade shows is to sell to the stores.

It's a good idea to have tear sheets of your work—like the one pictured here—and a business card to leave with the art director. You can always follow up with a phone call later.

Louie Award Winner

© Renaissance Greeting Cards, Inc.
Created by Sherry Schmidt
B.D. Fox Supergroup

This is an example of a tearsheet. You can have a professional printer make a tearsheet of your work, but it's expensive. A more cost-effective way is to make your own with a color copier. Use high-quality paper and go to a copy store that has good equipment and a knowledgeable staff. Use samples of your best work.

Trade Publications

The three major trade publications are *Greetings etc.*, *GSB* and *Giftware News.* I highly recommend subscribing to them. Not only can you use them to find contacts, but they provide a wealth of information on trends.

Just as there are trends in fashion, there are trends in card design. In fact, the card industry is very trend-oriented and driven. The sunflower motif was hot in the early 1990s. Angels came next. So what's popular now? What's next? You'll find the answers in the trade publications.

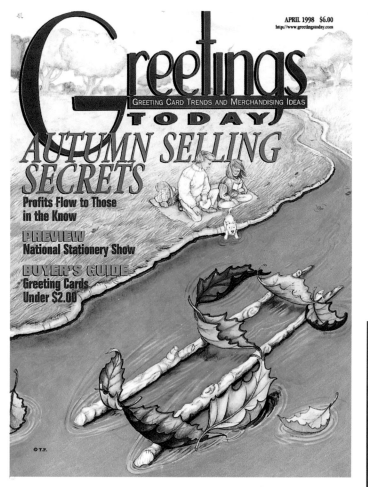

TRADE PUBLICATION INFORMATION

- *Greetings etc.*, the official publication of the Greeting Card Association, is published by Edgell Publications, Inc., 10 W. Hanover Avenue, Suite 107, Randolph, NJ 07869-4214; (973) 895-3300.
- *GSB*, 600 Harrison Street, San Francisco, CA 94107.
- *Giftware News*, 20 N. Wacker Drive, Suite 3230, Chicago, IL 60606; (312) 849-2220.

More Research Ideas

Another source to aid your research is the *Artist's & Graphic Designer's Market* published by Writer's Digest Books. An entire section is devoted to greeting cards, gifts and products. Listings give the company name, address, number of years it's been in business, the owner's or art director's name, the type of art they buy, how and/or what they pay and other useful information.

Some artists have found greeting card companies on the Internet. They are also listed on the CD-ROM of American businesses.

ROBERTSON'S COTTAGE
© *Notations*
From an original by Jeanette Robertson

BENCH
© *Notations*
From an original by Jeanette Robertson

How to Approach Card Companies

Resumes, Query Letters and Tearsheets

Even if you haven't sold any art to card companies, you'll need a resume to send to them. There are a number of great resume writing books on the market that I recommend you look at. Remember that the card company will be particularly interested in your art background.

QUERY LETTER

A query letter is a letter to an art director requesting information about their art needs. You set up a query letter just like any other business letter. Be concise, but friendly. Be sure to find out the art director's name and send it directly to her. Provide a brief background about yourself and include a sample of your art style—a tearsheet like the one here would be a good sample. You can ask specific questions, but they may not be answered directly. Usually all of the information you need to know will be in the guidelines when you receive them.

Jeanette Robertson

Cazenovia, NY 13035

Art Guidelines

You may request artist's guidelines from one or many companies. Once you receive them, study them. Become familiar with what they want: what colors, what subjects, what mediums.

If they mention a pay scale, ask yourself if you're satisfied with what they pay. If not, look for another company.

As a beginner, you will most likely sell on speculation, which means doing a design on your own and then trying to find a company that will buy it. Sometimes you'll sell and sometimes you won't. At times it simply depends on the timing. But don't be discouraged. You have to keep at it.

ASSIGNMENTS

Once a company has purchased your work a few times and is familiar with your style, you may get an assignment asking you to do a specific design. They'll give you a due date, and you must submit your work before or on time. Then you'll be paid. If they're not satisfied with what you have done, you may be asked to make some changes. If this doesn't work out and the assignment is scrapped, most companies will give you a *kill fee*, which is compensation for your time, but not the full amount of pay you would have received if the artwork had been accepted. It's best to be gracious and accept the fee. The next project may work out fine.

SIZE OF WORK

You'll find most guidelines require the final artwork to be quite small. Most of my designs fit onto 8½″ × 11″ paper. This makes filing and mailing very easy. And for artists with limited storage space, this is great!

Some companies will want the artwork to be the same size as the actual card. However, most will let you work a little larger.

In chapter three, four companies and their guidelines will be profiled. Guidelines are fairly standard.

DON'T GIVE UP

I once had an assignment that I had to paint over and over again. In the end, they decided not to buy it and I received a kill fee. A year or two later, I sold them a design on speculation that became one of their best-sellers! So you never know!

Technical Considerations

There's a whole language to be aware of when working with the production of greeting cards and note cards. Here are some of the main technical terms you should be aware of.

Crop Marks

Crop marks, or crop lines, mark the position of the artwork on the card. Sometimes by just looking at the artwork, it's not clear where the art should be placed on the card. So the crop marks serve as guides.

Place your crop marks outside the artwork in pencil only. The lines shouldn't touch the art. Be aware that there are times when an art director may change the crop. When a design has an irregular shape or needs special placement, it might look like the card on this page.

Artwork with crop marks showing where the art will be positioned on the card.

The front of the actual card.

© Gina B. Designs, Inc.
Original watercolor by Gina Bugee Karl

Full Bleed

The term *full bleed* is used to indicate that the artwork completely covers the front of the card.

Artwork cropped to indicate full bleed.

The actual card.

ROBERTSON'S BEACH
© Cape Shore, Inc.
From an original design by Jeanette Robertson

Borders

You may be asked to create a border around your design. If a border is indicated, it would look like these cards.

Artwork with crops for a border.

The actual card.

THE AMERICA
Published by Cape Shore, Inc.
© Geraldine Aikman

Here are two cards published by the same company. They were presented for sale in two different ways and sizes.

ADIRONDACK CHAIRS
© *Notations*
From an original by Jeanette Robertson

ARBOR
© *Notations*
From an original by Jeanette Robertson

Roughs

Designs to show placement, colors or orientation are called *roughs*. An art director will often choose a final design from a number of roughs.

Example of a rough.

WINTER BEACH
© *Cape Shore, Inc.*
From an original design by Jeanette Robertson

Protect Your Art

When you send your original artwork to an art director, it's important to protect the work from handling. This can be done very simply. Use a sheet of tracing paper that is larger than the art. Place it over the art and then fold the excess over the top and to the back of the art. Use masking tape to fasten the tracing paper to the back of the art. Then trim the tracing paper around the art on the other three sides.

Cover the front of the artwork with a sheet of tracing paper.

Back of the Art
Fold the tracing paper around to the back of the art. Tape it with masking tape. Write your name, address and phone number on the back of the art.

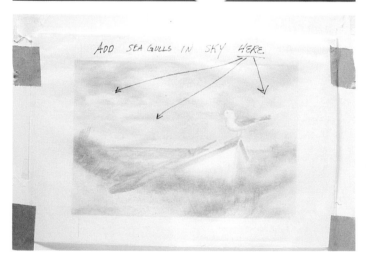

Another reason to use tracing paper over your art is so the art director can make notations on it. She may write directions about cropping and other production concerns for in-house use on it. She may also write changes she wants you to make to the art on the overlay.

Put Together a Portfolio

This is not something to fear! I've met so many artists who panic over the idea of putting together a portfolio. If you approach this as something that can be fun, you'll have a better time developing it.

To put together your portfolio, select ten to twelve of your best pieces of art. If you work in more than one medium, show a few samples of each. Design your art in card size and format. If you're fortunate to live near a card company, you can personally show the art director your original art. But if you're mailing your portfolio, which is the most common practice, make color copies of your art. *Do not send original art.* Some companies may request slides, but most will accept color copies.

Mail your portfolio in a large envelope. Use a folder with pockets to hold your color copies, letter and business card. Don't forget to enclose a self-addressed stamped envelope large enough to hold your portfolio when it is returned. Make sure to have the proper postage on both envelopes.

MULTIPLE SALES

When you sell your design to a company, they usually want to own the copyright outright. You can, however, arrange to give them the rights for the use as a card only. This gives you the freedom to sell the design to another company for a different product use, such as a mug, T-shirt, calendar and so on. You can't sell the use of the same design to more than one company for the same use. You need to work out each sale accordingly.

Your portfolio can consist of ten to twelve pieces of your best work. Use color copies to introduce your work to a new company.

Special Designs

I want to briefly touch on three types of card design: die cutting, foil-stamping and embossing. Each company will have a separate set of artist's guidelines for these types of cards. Generally, more seasoned artists will work on these projects.

© *Renaissance Greeting Cards, Inc.*
Design by Kate Beetle

Die Cutting

Die cutting is a technique in which a design is cut in the paper using a die. Sometimes it can be an outline cut around a subject, or a "window" cut into the cover with another image designed on the inside of the card.

Example of the die-cutting technique.

© *Renaissance Greeting Cards, Inc.*
Design by Jane Elizabeth McIlvain

Foil-Stamping

Foil-stamping adds a shiny, metallic look and is a printing technique that releases foil from its backing when stamped with a heated die. It can be done in many colors besides the traditional gold and silver.

© *Renaissance Greeting Cards, Inc.*
Design by Kate Beetle

Embossing

Embossing is a raised surface in the paper that is incorporated into the design. It can be as simple as a border or as detailed as a total design.

Example of embossing.

© *Renaissance Greeting Cards, Inc.*
Design by Jane Harding Whittle

"Tulips"

Deborah H. Rogers 98

SKATING ON CAZENOVIA LAKE

chapter three

Card Company Profiles

In this chapter, art directors from four card companies will

share information about what their companies need and

some samples of their final products.

Downeast Concepts, Inc.

Yarmouth, Maine
Anne W. Macleod, Art Director of Special Markets

Downeast Concepts, the parent company of Cape Shore, Inc. and Notations, produces mostly boxed note and Christmas cards. However, these are not their only products. They have a wide range of items that includes mugs, magnets, address books, photo albums, coasters, beverage napkins, gift items and more.

The company buys approximately fifty to sixty designs a year from freelance artists for their special markets line. The mediums they buy are watercolor, gouache, colored pencil and acrylic.

Be prepared to send samples of your work for company review, but don't expect a lot of positive or negative criticism from the art directors. They work hard under tight deadlines and really don't have time to critique each artist's work. So work in your own style, and don't give up.

Guidelines

The designs that sell best for Downeast Concepts are tightly rendered, traditional subjects such as florals, animals, birds, nautical themes and Christmas themes.

When designing with a full bleed, add ⅜″ on all sides so there's room to crop. Vertical or horizontal formats are fine.

The final card is a 67 percent reduction from the original art. The various styles are:

	FINAL ART	PRINTED PRODUCT
Note Cards	7⅞″ × 5½″	5¼″ × 3¹¹⁄₁₆″
Christmas Cards		
3000 Series	7⅞″ × 5½″	5¼″ × 3¹¹⁄₁₆″
4000 Series	9⅜″ × 6¾″	6¼″ × 4½″
5000 Series	8¾″ × 5⅞″	5⅞″ × 3¹⁵⁄₁₆″
6000 Series	9¾″ × 6¾″	6⁹⁄₁₆″ × 4⁷⁄₁₆″

All designs are submitted upon speculation. Artwork is purchased outright and may appear on one or more products. Send samples in a SASE.

PERCENTAGE WHEEL

A percentage wheel is a necessary tool for designing greeting cards. If an art director gives you the finished size of a card and tells you to render your artwork 30 percent, 67 percent of 75 percent larger, you can determine the dimensions for your original by using the percentage wheel. You can purchase one at most art supply stores.

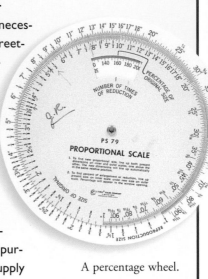

A percentage wheel.

Downeast Concepts Cards

TOPIARY
© *Notations*
From an original design by Jeanette Robertson

SUMMER LIGHT
© *Cape Shore, Inc.*
From an original design by
Kristin Stashenko

JEANETTE'S BEACH
© *Notations*
From an original by Jeanette
Robertson

REINDEER
© *Cape Shore, Inc.*
From an original design by Dawn Peterson

GARDENING
Published by Cape Shore, Inc.
© *Geraldine Aikman, Artist*

BEACHSIDE BUFFET
© Cape Shore, Inc.
From an original design by Jeanette Robertson

JEANETTE'S WINDOW BOX
© Notations
From an original by Jeanette Robertson

SUMMER BASKET
© Notations
From an original by Jeanette Robertson

Gina B. Designs, Inc.

Plymouth, Minnesota
Gina B. Karl, President

Gina Karl is an artist success story. She started her business in 1984 in the basement of her home, hand-painting floral designs on card stock and selling them to local stores. Because of their acceptance, she printed her first twelve designs—a run of 32,000 cards!

Gina credits her early success to local retailers. They helped her with design theme ideas, pricing and finding sales reps.

Guidelines

First become familiar with this company's style so your designs will complement their line. They prefer impressionistic watercolor florals and garden themes.

Contact them with a sample of your work in either color slides, photocopies or photos. Include a SASE for a reply and the return of your samples. Finished art should be 4″×5″ or 5″×7″. They buy twenty to thirty designs a year.

© Gina B. Designs, Inc.
Original watercolor by Gina Bugee Karl

Gina B. Designs Cards

© Gina B. Designs, Inc.
Original watercolor by Gina Bugee Karl

© Gina B. Designs, Inc.
Original watercolor by Christine Kenny

© Gina B. Designs, Inc.
Original watercolor by Gina Bugee Karl

with sympathy

with sympathy

Kristin Elliott, Inc.

Newburyport, Massachusetts
Barbara Elliott, Art Director

Kristin Elliott is a two-generation, family-owned business. It began as a home-based Christmas card company in which all four children assisted in assembling the product on the family's Ping-Pong table. Other products were added as the company grew.

Today the company offers boxed note cards, imprintables, photocards, greeting cards, Christmas cards, gift enclosures and tags. Recently journals and computer mouse pads were added. They rely solely on freelance artists. The emphasis is "Yankee value with exceptional product quality and superlative service."

Guidelines

They buy approximately two hundred designs per year, mostly watercolor. Very white, pliable, smooth paper stock is required. Clean, crisp colors are essential. Art may be done in a proportion of the final size.

Illustrative, graphic and whimsical styles are all used. Preferred subjects are music, golf, tennis and florals.

All designs are submitted on speculation and are reviewed all year, with January to May being the best time to submit. Send color photocopies or photos. Assignments are only given once a relationship is established. The company purchases the art outright and the artist is given credit on the back of the card. A SASE should be included with each submission.

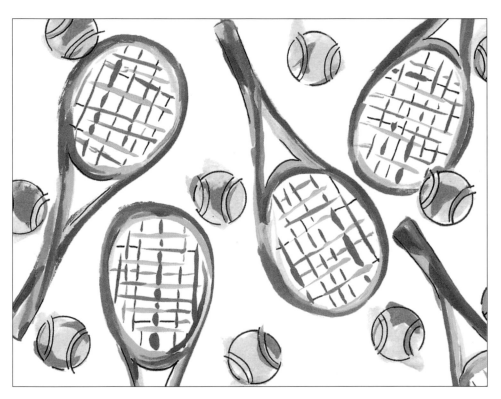

©Kristin Elliott, Inc.
Design by Linda Malkus Easler

Kristin Elliott Cards

©Kristin Elliott, Inc.
Design by Grace Tulpa Chase

©Kristin Elliott, Inc.
Design by Carla S. Koch

© Kristin Elliott, Inc.
Design by Richard J. Tardiff

© Kristin Elliott, Inc.
Design by Kristin Stashenko

© Kristin Elliott, Inc.
Design by Jeanette Robertson

© Kristin Elliott, Inc.
Design by Richard J. Tardiff

Renaissance Greeting Cards, Inc.

Springvale, Maine
Janice Keefe, Art Director

Renaissance Greeting Cards, Inc., a subsidiary of FTD, began twenty years ago in Turner Falls, Massachusetts, when a group of friends got together to make Christmas cards. They were members of a community called Renaissance, formed in the 1960s. The first six cards they printed were black-and-white Christmas cards, which were so popular that this company was formed.

"We wanted a better quality of life back then, and the honesty, integrity and high principles of that era have been the keys to our success," says cofounder and president Randy Kleinrock. The company follows a mission statement with the goal of "enhancing the quality of life: for both customers and employees." It's the only greeting card company to print everything—cards, boxes, stationery and catalogs—on recycled paper with vegetable-based inks.

By 1979, Renaissance was distributing color cards and receiving responses nationally. By 1985, over five million cards were distributed each year. Today the company has 750 everyday cards and 500 seasonally active designs, and annually distributes eight million cards.

Another market segment that Renaissance has occupied for a number of years is the cause-related niche. In addition to its pioneering use of recycled materials and vegetable-based inks, the company markets its Thanksgiving Day cards with a percentage of sales going to organizations that fight hunger. Other lines assist groups concerned with women's health issues.

Randy Kleinrock believes that greeting cards will easily survive the computer age. There's nothing that can replace the feeling of getting a card in the mail and knowing that someone went to the trouble of finding and sending a special card just for you. It's tangible and lasts longer than a phone call.

Guidelines

Renaissance is interested in seeing innovative material, trendy themes and styles, sophisticated art, well-executed designs, images that communicate, and occasion-oriented designs, as well as upbeat, humorous material.

Designs are purchased on speculation and from assignments. They buy worldwide rights to the artwork. Paper must be of a flexible stock. Mediums can be watercolor, pastel, colored pencil, gouache, illustrators dyes and so on. A vertical format is preferred with designs done in the actual size of $5\frac{1}{8}'' \times 7\frac{1}{2}''$ or at 150 percent ($7\frac{11}{16}'' \times 11\frac{1}{8}''$) with $\frac{1}{8}''$ of color on all sides for bleeds. Adjust accordingly for larger art. For a border allowance, $\frac{3}{16}''$ of space is needed between the edge cut and image.

Designs are considered for Valentine's Day, spring and fall occasions, Christmas and Hanukkah, as well as specialty, all-occasion and humorous cards.

Please include postage-paid packaging for returning submissions, and allow six to eight weeks for a response.

Renaissance Cards

THROUGH THE YEARS
© Renaissance Greeting Cards, Inc.
By Jane Elizabeth McIlvain

PASSOVER
© Renaissance
Greeting Cards, Inc.
Image by Kate Beetle

MAGIC OF LIFE
© Renaissance Greeting Cards, Inc.
By Jane Elizabeth McIlvain

FATHER'S DAY
© *Renaissance Greeting Cards, Inc.*
Image by Kate Beetle

BIRTHDAY/FATHER
© *Renaissance Greeting Cards, Inc.*
Image by Jane Harding Whittle

LOVE'S BLOSSOM
© *Renaissance Greeting Cards, Inc.*
By Jane Harding Whittle

SOOTHING HERBAL WISHES
© Renaissance Greeting Cards, Inc.
Created by Sherry Schmidt
B.D. Fox Supergroup

TIMELESS TREASURE
© Renaissance Greeting Cards, Inc.
By Jane Harding Whittle

With sympathy and friendship...

thank you

chapter four

Design and Paint Cards Step by Step

Every card artist's story is as unique as one's own fingerprints.

In this chapter, you'll see a variety of styles, subjects and

mediums as successful greeting card artists share tips, encour-

agement and step-by-step demonstrations of their cards.

Some of the artists do freelance work with card companies

and others publish their own art as cards.

Geraldine Aikman
Likes Short-Term Projects

Geraldine Aikman is a freelance illustrator and a graduate of Paier College of Art in Connecticut. She works mostly in ink, watercolor and gouache.

She originally studied to be a children's book illustrator. However, once she worked in greeting cards, she found the short-term assignments suited her better. She began freelancing in the early 1980s after acquiring a copy of the *Artist's Market* and quickly gained work from inquiries she made using that resource.

Tips to Artists

Geraldine recommends that you follow the directions given to you from the art director. Be neat, accurate and prompt—these are important factors.

Never sell more rights than the client needs. Get reuse fees from companies who manufacture a variety of products.

Keep good records on every job.

MATERIALS

For this design called *Windy Day*, Geraldine used Strathmore Bristol 3-ply regular surface paper. She prefers Winsor & Newton Designers' Gouache. For brushes, she likes Winsor & Newton Scepter Gold Series nos. 00 to 2. She uses Scotch masking tape #234.

Have you been to sea on a windy day
When the ocean is blue
And the sky is too...

WINDY DAY
Published by Cape Shore, Inc.
© *Geraldine Aikman*

Title: 'Windy Day'
Final Art: 6¾ x 9⅜ (plus 3/16" bleed)
Card size: 4½ x 6¼
Medium: Gouache on
Strathmore Bristol
Regular Surface
3-ply

• Higher central image
• Thin blue line

• Vertical
• No blue line

• top floral sprigs larger
• central image lower
• wider blue border

Step 1

When Geraldine receives an assignment, it tells her the size, subject matter and particulars of what the card company wants. In this case, they want a New England coastline scene in the center of a card with a white border that includes flowers and berries. She is instructed to leave space for text, which they'll fill in later.

Working within these guidelines, she makes three color sketches proportional to but smaller than the size of the finished card, and submits the sketches to the art director. She gets the OK to do a final drawing of sketch #2.

ART: 6¾ x 9⅜

Step 2

Geraldine completes the drawing in the final art size using pencil on tracing paper. She makes a copy and faxes it to the art director for approval. Approval arrives and she receives her deadline, which is in fourteen days.

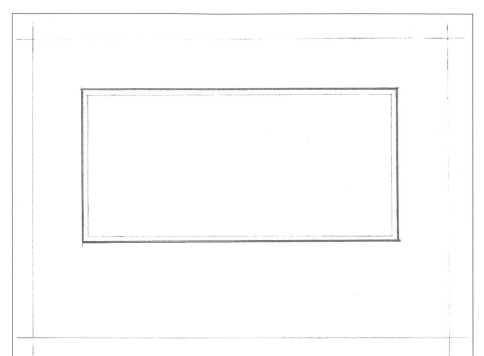

Step 3

Geraldine uses Strathmore Bristol 3-ply regular surface paper and a 2B soft lead mechanical pencil to begin the card. First she draws lines to show the edges of the drawing and the rectangle in the center. With a ruling pen, she first lines the thin, blue border using watered-down gouache.

When this is dry, she transfers her drawing by using tracing paper with graphite applied and rubbed in. This makes a light transfer, so it's easy to erase.

Step 4

Next she masks around the central image with Scotch masking tape #234, and puts tracing paper under the tape as a splatter guard. She alternates painting the central picture and the corner sprigs, beginning with the sprigs. Starting at the top of the central image, she paints in the sky and blocks in the grassy foreground. When finished, she removes the tape and touches up any irregularities with white gouache right out of the tube.

Step 5

Geraldine tapes the art onto white board and protects it by placing tracing paper over it. She makes color copies for her records, and then packs the art between two pieces of stiff cardboard and sends it to the card company.

Geraldine makes an invoice and log sheet for every piece of art. On the log sheet is a record of the start and finish dates, the date she sends the art, the company name, the art director's name, her fee, the product usage and any miscellaneous notes pertaining to the project. At the bottom of the log, she notes when the card is scheduled to be printed, and the dates she receives her sample cards and her original art is returned.

More Cards by Geraldine Aikman

HARVEST HOUSE
Published by Cape Shore, Inc.
© Geraldine Aikman

SHE SELLS
SEA SHELLS
THANK YOU
Published by Cape Shore, Inc.
© Geraldine Aikman

AMERICAN FLAG
© *Notations*
From an original by Geraldine Aikman

NAUTICAL VILLAGE
Published by Cape Shore, Inc.
© *Geraldine Aikman*

David Hughes
An American Success Story

David Hughes, president of David Hughes Watercolors, decided to try his hand at the greeting card business in 1990 after receiving encouragement from his family and friends. He started by selling to local shops where his cards were received with enthusiasm. In the beginning, the cards cost more than they sold for, but he quickly learned there was a considerable market for his work.

In 1991, he exhibited at the National Stationery Show and in the Atlanta Gift Show. Orders came in, sales reps were enthusiastic about his work and within a year he had about one hundred fifty customers throughout the eastern United States. Along the way David learned how to get his printing costs down so he could make a profit.

David Hughes Watercolors now sells its cards and prints in over one thousand stores throughout the U.S. and in a few foreign countries. His cards are marketed mainly through sales representatives. He tries to add eight new designs to the line each year. Store owners report that their customers buy these uniquely American cards to frame (for themselves or as gifts) as much as they do to mail.

THE CARRIAGE
David Hughes
Photograph by Tee Adams, Paoli, PA

Step 1

David first draws the carriage design in pencil. Using liquid mask, he masks out the birch trees along with most of the carriage. He uses Winsor & Newton watercolor Cerulean Blue with Winsor & Newton Chinese White as a wash over the sky; Thalo Blue by Grumbacher Academy for the distant trees; Yellow Ochre by Winsor & Newton in the field; and Cadmium Red by Winsor & Newton in a few bushes.

Step 2

He paints the branch areas with washes of bluish gray. Then he roughs in a horizontal row of bushes using Vandyke Brown, Raw Umber and Burnt Umber by Winsor & Newton. The more detailed areas to the field are done with Vandyke Brown.

Step 3

He develops the painting more using the same colors as in step 1. As he works, David feels something of interest is needed at the right center and decides a lake will provide more color and interest. So in it goes, using a variety of blues. His subjects are rarely identifiable places, so if he wants to add a lane, a body of water or even a shed, he does it.

Step 4

David adds the final details with the same colors used in the other steps. For additional interest, he adds some wildflowers.

COTSWALD COTTAGE
David Hughes
Photograph by Tee Adams, Paoli, PA

Step 1
David uses liquid mask on the blossoms and then applies washes for the sky using Indigo by Winsor & Newton and Chinese White by Winsor & Newton Cotman. He uses Winsor & Newton Yellow Ochre for the cottage and stone fences, and Hooker's Green and Phthalo Green for the bushes and grass.

Step 2
David then adds the roof detail with Raw Umber and Burnt Umber. He does the background trees with Hooker's Green and Cerulean Blue, and paints the stone walls in with Lamp Black by Winsor & Newton and washes of Yellow Ochre. He also paints a few blossoms in Cadmium Red.

Step 3
Using colors from the other steps, David adds details to the garden, lawn structures and cottage.

Step 4

He accents the door with Thalo Blue and gray, and also uses gray on the stone steps. He paints the blossoms in Cadmium Red and Cerulean Blue, and finishes the walls and iron fence.

More Cards by David Hughes

ADIRONDACK
CHAIRS
David Hughes
Watercolor

COUNTRY GEMS
David Hughes
Watercolor

ROADSIDE CRAFTS
David Hughes
Watercolor

THE CHRISTMAS TREE
David Hughes
Watercolor

SPRING IS HERE
David Hughes
Watercolor

Jane Harding Whittle
A Backyard Artist

In 1978, Jane Whittle received her bachelor of fine arts from Northern Kentucky University. She majored in printmaking and drawing. Today she works in colored pencil.

It took a full year of making contacts by mail for Jane to start selling her cards as a freelancer. In that time she learned an important lesson. You can't be hardheaded when contacting a company! She realized that what she liked to draw and what the companies wanted to buy was not always the same. Now she only sends her work to companies that she knows publish her style.

Most of her images are very personal to her. She finds plants and animal subjects in her own backyard. Friends and family bring her shells, leaves and other assorted things to use as subjects for her art.

THANK-YOU
Image by Jane Harding Whittle
©Renaissance Greeting Cards, Inc.

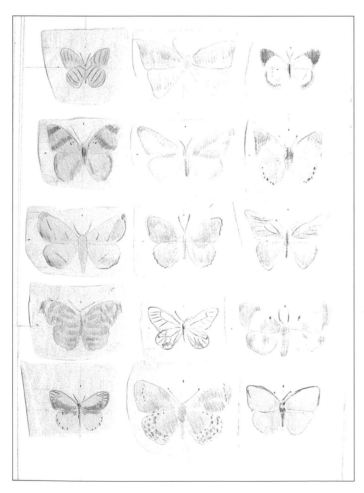

Step 1
Jane plans the entire card on a tracing layout first.

Step 2
One at a time, she draws and colors the butterflies. Here she lightly applies the first color.

Step 3
She lightly adds the second color.

Step 4
All of the colors are now deepened and one butterfly is complete.

Karol B. Wyckoff
Internationally Known

Karol Wyckoff has a bachelor of fine arts from the Rhode Island School of Design and studied at the Massachusetts School of Art and the Museum of Fine Arts in Boston. Watercolor is the medium she works in the most, although she sometimes works in oils and pastels.

She publishes her cards locally in Cape Cod, her hometown, where they've been marketed for many years. Galleries first found her through her address on the back of her cards, and now her cards are distributed internationally.

STAGE HARBOR LIGHT
© Karol B. Wyckoff
Watercolor

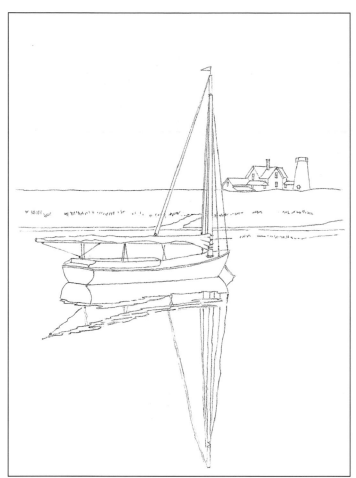

Step 1

After doing a series of thumbnail sketches to determine the composition and light patterns, Karol renders the drawing using a no. 2 pencil on Arches 300 lb. (640gsm) cold-press watercolor paper.

Step 2

Next, Karol blocks out the areas that need to remain the white of the paper by using liquid mask. Then, using a flat 1-inch bristle brush, she wets the sky and pond areas with clear water. Mixing Cerulean Blue, Winsor Violet and a touch of Burnt Sienna, she selectively drops the colors into the wet areas with a no. 10 Winsor & Newton Series 7 sable brush, controlling the placement to achieve soft flows of color. Once these areas dry, she wets the grass area with clear water and adds a light combination of Raw Sienna and Prussian Blue, once again controlling the paint flow.

KAROL B. WYCKOFF

Step 3

Once dry with the help of a hair dryer, Karol rewets the grass area with clear water and adds more color for contrast using the same colors as in step 2. While this is drying, she uses a no. 2 Series 7 sable brush to paint the reflection of the sailboat. To complete the mast and boat trim, she uses a combination of Raw Umber and Burnt Sienna. Winsor Violet with a dab of Burnt Sienna and Raw Umber finishes off the starboard side and the stern of the boat. When all is bone dry, she removes the liquid mask with a rubber cement eraser.

Step 4

In the final stages, Karol paints the details of the lighthouse using nos. 1 and 2 Series 7 sable brushes. She uses a touch of Rose Madder Genuine, Winsor Violet and Burnt Umber for the roof, and uses the same palette from the shadow of the boat for the shaded light of the buildings. Karol adds a touch of Aureolin for the windows. She finishes the boat with the same palette as the reflection of the boat, with the exception of the Cerulean Blue flag. She paints the stays with a no. 2 rigger brush using Vandyke Brown and Prussian Blue. In all cases, Winsor & Newton Artists' professional tube watercolors and Winsor & Newton Series 7 sable brushes are used.

More Cards by Karol B. Wyckoff

BEACH ROSES
© *Karol B. Wyckoff*

MISTY MARSH
© *Karol B. Wyckoff*

BLUE MOON
© *Karol B. Wyckoff*

UNCLE TIM'S
BRIDGE
© *Karol B. Wyckoff*

COUNTRY STORE
© *Karol B. Wyckoff*

OLD GLORY
© *Karol B. Wyckoff*

BEACON HILL FLURRIES
© *Karol B. Wyckoff*

Barbara Schaffer
Small World

Barbara Schaffer's art education is from the School of Art and Design and the Art Students League, both in New York City. She works in all mediums except oils.

She's designed cards for twenty-five years. She worked as an art director for a major card company and when that company moved to another state, she decided to freelance her work. She obtains most of her work from stationery shows and works with an art agent.

SANTA ON BEACH
©Barbara Schaffer

Step 1
Using black waterproof India ink in a Rapidograph pen, Barbara first does a pen-and-ink outline on Strathmore 500 Series Bristol, 3-ply regular finish cold-press paper.

Step 2

She then uses Winsor & Newton Series 7 sable round brushes nos. 2, 3, 5 and 8 to apply the first colors: Peacock Blue for the sky, Cyprus Green for the ocean, and Yellow Ochre for the sand.

Step 3

She adds Brilliant Green, Cadmium Red Medium and Yellow Ochre to the tree, packages and Santa, and completes the other details with Burnt Sienna.

Step 4

Barbara paints the sun with Permanent Yellow, the reindeer with Burnt Sienna and adds the finishing touches.

CAT BAND
Barbara Schaffer

Step 1

Once again, Barbara uses black waterproof India ink in a Rapidograph pen to draw the outline. Her paper is Strathmore 500 Series Bristol, 3-ply regular finish cold-press.

Step 2

Barbara uses Ultramarine Blue in the background, Permanent Green and Brilliant Green on the holly, Lamp Black in the music notes and Cadmium Red Medium on the holly berries. She does the shading with a blend of Lamp Black and Peacock Blue.

Step 3

She paints each cat a different color, using Lamp Black, Yellow Ochre, Burnt Sienna and Permanent Yellow.

Step 4

Finally, Barbara paints the musical instruments with Yellow Ochre, Burnt Sienna and a blend of Lamp Black with Burnt Sienna.

Veronica Reid Johanns
Loves Children

Veronica Johanns has a bachelor of fine arts from Alfred University. She's designed cards for seven years and works primarily in pen and ink and watercolor. Childrens' themes are her most recent interest. She sells her hand-painted cards at arts and crafts shows, in gift shops and galleries and by catalog.

For the design described here, a black-and-white outline was preprinted onto watercolor paper sheets. She then hand-painted the individual motifs in color. A unique aspect of her cards is that she cuts out each character and glues them onto the preprinted background using thin cardboard to give the motifs a two-dimensional look. She mixes and matches different motifs, so each card is one-of-a-kind.

RONI'S ART ORIGINALS
By Veronica Reid Johanns

Step 1
Using a Grumbacher no. 0 round brush, Veronica prepares to paint the first motif. She first draws the designs on the watercolor paper with a Rapidograph pen size 1.35 nib using waterproof black ink.

Step 2
Using Winsor & Newton watercolor paint, she applies the first four colors—Cadmium Yellow, Burnt Sienna, Indigo Blue and Cadmium Scarlet.

Step 3
Veronica adds Spectrum Violet, Cadmium Yellow Deep, Payne's Gray and Alizarin Crimson mixed with white to the next motifs.

Step 4
In the next few motifs, she uses Hooker's Green, Payne's Gray, Raw Sienna, Lamp Black and Cadmium Red.

Step 5
After all of the motifs on the paper are painted, Veronica begins to cut out the objects.

Step 6
She carefully cuts out each motif, trimming off any excess paper.

Step 7

Next, she cuts a small piece of cardboard or mat board and glues it to the back of each motif. This is what is unique about Veronica's cards—they are dimensional.

Step 8

Veronica glues the motifs onto a card that is pre-drawn with pen-and-ink designs that create a great background for the characters. Notice how the shadows add interest to the card.

Gail Roth
Card Companies Found Her

Gail Roth is a graduate of the Paier School of Art. She works in both watercolor and colored pencil.

She's worked as an illustrator for ten years, and her work has been published in *Country Living* magazine. A card company art director saw her art and asked her to create some cards for them. The more work she did, the more she found. It snowballed from there! She now sells her designs to companies that market nationwide.

©idesign greeting cards, inc.
Art by Gail Roth

Step 1
First, Gail completes a detailed pencil drawing using a Staedtler/Mars mechanical pencil with HB leads on Fabriano 140 lb. (300gsm) hot-press watercolor paper.

Step 2

To get a feel for the overall color scheme, Gail washes a hint of color over the paper. She uses a Winsor & Newton Cotman #222 no. 4 round brush with Winsor & Newton watercolors: Winsor Emerald, Alizarin Crimson and Naples Yellow.

Step 3

Using a no. 2 brush, Gail adds shadows using Payne's Gray. She adds the first shadows to the hat box and hearts, making the objects look round and plump, and adds more colors all over using Cobalt Violet, Ultramarine Blue, Sap Green and more Alizarine Crimson with touches of Cadmium Scarlet.

Step 4

Gail uses deeper values of all the colors from steps 2 and 3 to make the objects take on more shape. Her last touch is adding Prismacolor colored pencils for texture and definition. The pencil colors she uses are Dark Green, Celadon Green, Marine Green, Ultramarine Blue, Pink Rose and Tuscan Red.

More Cards by Gail Roth

The fronts and backs of many of Gail's cards are all works of art.

© Gail Roth

© Gail Roth

© Gail Roth

© Gail Roth

Dawn Peterson
Lifelong Love of Nature

Dawn Peterson, who works mostly in watercolor, studied painting at the Art Students League in New York City.

In addition to greeting cards, her artwork has appeared in magazines and books, and she has illustrated five childrens' books, including childrens' books sold by L.L. Bean. She's lived in the woods and countryside of several states, where she developed a love of nature. She now resides in coastal Maine.

MATERIALS

Dawn likes to use Winsor & Newton tube watercolors, Winsor & Newton Series 7 round sable brushes from no. 000 to no. 3. She also uses a 2-inch flat sable brush. For paper, Arches 300 lb. (640gsm) cold-press is her favorite.

GOLD FINCHES

© *Cape Shore, Inc.*

From an original design by Dawn Peterson

Step 1

Dawn plans the outside dimension around the client's size specification. Using an H lead mechanical drawing pencil, she draws the outline on Arches 300 lb. (640gsm) cold-press watercolor paper.

Step 2

She applies color to the finches using a Winsor & Newton Series 7 no. 3 brush and Winsor Yellow with a touch of Winsor & Newton Gamboge.

Step 3

Dawn then adds Raw Umber, Gamboge, Oxide of Chromium and Cadmium Yellow Light to the birds. She gives the thistle blossoms a wash of Alizarin Crimson with a touch of Winsor Violet, and makes the foliage with a combination of Oxide of Chromium, Cadmium Yellow Light and Ultramarine Blue.

Step 4

She paints all of the black areas of the birds with a mixture of French Ultramarine and Warm Sepia. For the beaks and feet, she uses Light Red, Gamboge and a touch of Burnt Sienna. Dawn gives the thistle blossoms more detail in both the pink and green areas, and does a little outlining with Warm Sepia. She completes the tiny details with a no. 000 round brush.

More Cards by Dawn Peterson

BUNNY TRIO
© Notations
From an original by Dawn Peterson

THE ANIMALS CHRISTMAS
© Cape Shore, Inc.
From an original design by Dawn Peterson

ORCAS
©*Cape Shore, Inc.*
From an original design by
Dawn Peterson

THE KEEPERS LIGHT
©*Cape Shore, Inc.*
From an original by Dawn Peterson

Amy Farry
One of My Students

Amy works in watercolors and has a bachelor of fine arts from Alfred University. She has a full-time job outside of fine art, but spends her free time working at her art. She painted the sunflowers described here for my greeting card class and will be contacting companies to sell this design and others.

MATERIALS

Amy uses Winsor & Newton Artists' professional watercolors in tubes. Her brushes are a 1-inch flat brush Series 700 by Royal, and nos. 2 and 6 rounds by Princeton Art and Brush Company Series 4350R. The paper she uses is Arches 140 lb. (300gsm) hot-press. She adds touches of texture with Staedtler watercolor pencils.

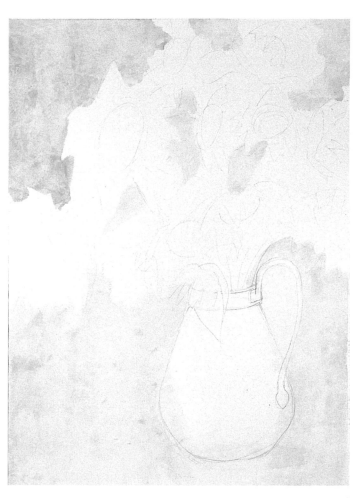

Step 1
Amy first draws a light pencil layout and puts a light color wash on the background using Cadmium Red Pale Hue.

Step 2
She paints the sunflowers with Cadmium Yellow Pale Hue, the stems with Hooker's Green, the centers of the flowers with Burnt Umber and the vase with a wash of Prussian Blue.

Step 3
Amy adds shadows with a blend of Prussian Blue and Cadmium Red Pale Hue. She adds more Hooker's Green to the stems, Sepia to the center of the flowers and Burnt Sienna to the yellow of the flowers.

Step 4
To punch up the color, Amy uses a deeper value of all the colors in the previous steps. For a little texture and definition, she adds colored pencil.

SUNFLOWERS
Amy Farry

Kristin Stashenko
Persistence Pays Off

Kristin Stashenko, who has been designing cards for about five years, majored in illustration at the Massachusetts College of Art. She also attended courses at the Boston Museum of Fine Arts.

After graduating college, her target market was the greeting card industry. She researched companies at card stores, chose a number of companies to approach and then sent them her portfolio. She got a lot of rejections, but her persistence paid off and she began to receive assignments. Now she freelances for eight companies and still searches out new prospects. She works mostly by assignment.

> **MATERIALS**
>
> Kristin uses Winsor & Newton 140 lb. (300gsm) hot-press paper. For brushes, she uses Winsor & Newton Scepter Gold Series nos. 2, 4 and 6 rounds.

Step 1
Using photos shot in Key West as references, Kristin first does a detailed drawing.

Step 2
Kristin paints the major shadows using a wet-in-wet technique. She lets the colors do their own mixing right on the paper from a combination of Ultramarine Blue, Mauve, Cobalt Violet and Cerulean Blue.

Step 3
Using Lemon Yellow Hue, Yellow Ochre and Cobalt Violet, she adds warm and midtone values. Kristin builds up the colors of the flowers in layers, from light to dark, using Cadmium Red, Permanent Rose, Winsor Green, Burnt Sienna and Sepia.

Step 4
She punches up all of the colors in the previous steps. This gives the work depth.

KEY WEST
Kristin Stashenko
Photograph by Joe Buchanan

Navina Capecci
Designing Cards for Thirty-Five Years

Navina Capecci studied art at various art schools in New York City. She works mostly in watercolor, gouache and colored pencil. Her first job after art school was at Norcross Inc., which was located in New York City. She now freelances her work.

Navina has a philosophy about art. "I believe the essence of the card subject determines the technique and handling. A flower's essence is its delicate, translucent quality. If it slides off the card and onto the floor, the sound would be silent and not a large clang."

> **MATERIALS**
>
> Navina uses Strathmore 3-ply medium finish paper. For brushes, she uses Winsor & Newton Series 7 nos. 0, 2 and 3. She uses Winsor & Newton watercolors and Designers' Gouache, and Eagle Verithin pencils for accents.

Step 1
First, Navina does a detailed drawing.

Step 2
She paints a rough color layout to plan the color balance of the entire piece.

Step 3
Navina begins the painting on Strathmore 3-ply medium finish paper. She uses Series 7 round brushes nos. 0, 2 and 3 throughout, and adds Winsor & Newton Designer colors a little at a time.

Step 4
She continues painting in color. The pale pink colors are Winsor Red and Zinc White. The cooler pink color is Rose Tyrien. The warm blues are a combination of Ultramarine Blue, Rose Tyrien and Zinc White. The centers of the pansies are Havanah Lake. The yellow is Cadmium Yellow. The greens are a variety of Olive Green, Sap Green, Winsor Green and Permanent Green. She also mixes some of the greens with white. Navina uses Eagle Verithin colored pencils for texture and definition.

FLORAL
Navina Capecci
Watercolor

Kate Beetle
Self-Starter

Kate Beetle, a self-taught artist, works mostly in watercolor, but also works in gouache, Prismacolor pencils, pastels and oils. Kate designed her first card in 1991 and sold it to Renaissance Cards. Since then they have purchased at least sixty-eight of her designs.

Since 1991, Kate has worked with an artist's agent, who finds assignments for her and charges Kate a percentage of the payment. Kate prefers not to do the selling herself, but realizes that selling is part of the business.

Kate's keys to artistic success are "sticking to it," and "practice, practice, practice." She encourages you to know your style and make a pilgrimage to the National Stationery Show in New York City.

When Kate has that occasional discouraged feeling, she pulls out all of her past work. Seeing her growth as an artist inspires her to keep working. In 1998, Kate won a Louie Award for her work.

She's also very organized and maintains extensive reference files. Since most cards are designed for holidays, she keeps separate files for each one, for example, filed under "Christmas" is a set of cultural icons and under "food" are photos of candy canes, ribbon candy, cookies, gingerbread, wassail, fruit, eggnog, fruitcakes . . . and that's just food!

Step 1
To plan out design and color relationships, Kate first does a very rough color sketch.

Step 2
After seeing the rough, Kate decides to change the border and make it less cluttered, so she does a detailed pencil drawing.

Step 3
She adds the colors to the drawing.

Step 4
Kate completes the design using the following colors: Rose Madder Genuine and Aureolin Yellow by Winsor & Newton; Cobalt Blue by Schmincke; Ultramarine, Phthalo Blue, Viridian and Cadmium Yellow Deep by Finest; Quinacridone Gold, Anthroquinoid Red, Pyrrol Red, Carbogole Violet, Indigo, Cobalt Violet and Quinacridone Rose by Daniel Smith.

FAVORITE MATERIALS

For *Eggs & Feathers* Kate used Strathmore 500, 3-ply bristol paper. Her brush here is Isabey 6227Z no. 4. Kate uses Winsor & Newton, Schmincke, Finest, and Daniel Smith paints in this design.

EGGS & FEATHERS
© *Renaissance Greeting Cards, Inc.*
Design by Kate Beetle

A Thank-You Card

I'll close this chapter with demonstrations of my own card designs.

Step 2
I render the design on Strathmore Bristol with a smooth surface. Prismacolor colored pencils are the colors in the letters and musical note. For interest, I make the letters light and dark within each letter so they won't look flat.

Step 1
I work on my lightbox for many of my designs. I find it's easier, faster and cleaner than drawing the outline on the final art. I simply place the art under the final paper and work on top of the outline. In the case of this thank-you card I use a computer printout of the words and hand-draw the musical note.

Step 3
I blend the colored pencil with a colorless Design Art Marker, giving the final art a smooth, finished look.

THANK-YOU
Jeanette Robertson

More Thank-You Cards

FLOWER BASKET
© Notations
From an original design by Jeanette Robertson

This was my original design for this card. The words "Thank You" were added by the card company. I didn't even know it until I received my sample cards!

SUNFLOWER &
BEE
© Notations
From an original design by Jeanette Robertson

Picket Fence

Step 1

I draw the fence, arbor and house in pencil on Arches 140 lb. (300gsm) cold-press watercolor paper. I save the important white areas with liquid mask.

Step 2

I add the sky and other base coats of color with a wet-in-wet method using Winsor & Newton tube paint. I warm up the paper with a little wash of Yellow Ochre in the sky and foreground. Then I add a Sap Green wash to the garden area. The sky is Prussian Blue.

Step 3

I remove the liquid mask; then I paint the garden area with French Ultramarine, Permanent Rose, Cadmium Yellow, Cadmium Scarlet, Sap Green, Sepia, Mauve, Hooker's Green and Payne's Gray.

I use all the colors as in step 3 to finish the design. Then I add texture to the side-walk and roof with a toothbrush stipple technique.

PICKET FENCE
©Notations
Jeanette Robertson

Snowman

Step 1

Using Arches 140 lb. (300gsm) cold-press watercolor paper, I do a basic pencil drawing of the major shapes. I use liquid mask to protect the areas that need to remain white, and a toothbrush to stipple in the mask for the snowflakes. The snowflakes will appear when the liquid mask is removed.

Step 2

I use Winsor & Newton French Ultramarine and Mauve to paint in the sky area. I blot up the ridge area where the trees will go.

Step 3

To make the shadows on the snow, I use Mauve with a little French Ultramarine. I add the trees with Hooker's Green and Payne's Gray. Once these are dry, I remove the liquid mask.

Step 4

I use Lamp Black for the hat and face and Sepia for the arms of the snowman. Cadmium Red Deep is used for the bird and scarf and Chrome Orange for the carrot nose. I paint the snowflakes on the scarf with white gouache.

SNOWMAN
Jeanette Robertson

Fish

Step 2
Then I take a long sheet of plastic wrap like the kind you use to wrap food. I crumple it up and lightly place it on top of my wet painted paper. I put this away and let it dry completely.

Step 1
This technique is a lot of fun because I don't know what will happen until the paper dries. The background is always an accident! First, I paint a very wet background. In this case, I used a solid color for an underwater scene, but multicolors can also be used for other subjects.

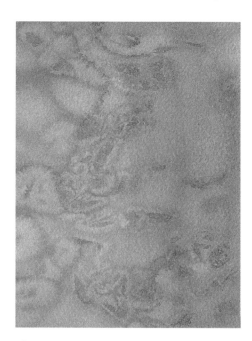

Step 3
When I remove the plastic wrap, I am left with an interesting pattern.

Step 4
Using gouache paint, which is opaque, I paint the fish designs right onto the background.

FISH
Jeanette Robertson

Roses on a Fence

This is from a photo I took in Nantucket one summer. I enlarged it on a regular black-and-white photocopier. This saves me a lot of time because I don't have to draw the entire design.

Step 2

I used the lightbox for this design too. First, I use a light pencil to mark out the areas of details that I'll need to use in the final steps. Since I don't want to do the entire art on the lightbox, I use pastel washes of gray on the house, blue in the sky, green behind the fence and pink in the roses.

Step 3

I use liquid mask on a small portion of the fence so I can put the detail texture on the house. I develop the design by using the same colors as in step 2 but deeper. I also add a little purple to have more colorful shadows than gray.

Step 4

I use deeper values of the same colors to develop the design even more. The glass in the windows reflects the colors in front of them. This gives the glass a real look and adds a little more warmth to the windows.

Step 5
Next, I add more color and more shadows. To give the subject a little more life, I add three birds in flight.

ROSES ON A FENCE
Jeanette Robertson

Sunset Beach

Step 1

I render a detailed pencil drawing of a storm fence on a beach on Arches 140 lb. (300gsm) cold-press paper. A pencil suggestion of the horizon, sand, dune and a few grasses is all that's needed for the beach. I pencil in the seagull and use liquid mask on the bird so it remains white.

Step 2

For this design, I use a watercolor pan paint by Pelikan, a German company. Since my palette is in German, I'll use the generic color name. First I wet the paper with clear water. Then I use yellow to warm up the paper in a few places in the sky and sand, and add pastel values of violet, magenta and turquoise blue in the sky and beach.

Step 4
Next, I render the details of the seagull and decide to add two gulls in the distance. I also add the wire to the fence with a dark gray. To stipple texture on the beach, I use a toothbrush.

SUNSET BEACH
Jeanette Robertson

Thank You

With caring
thoughts
and loving
wishes.

CHAMOMILE
COMFREY
LAVE

chapter five

Self-Publishing— Business Aspects

If you decide to self-publish rather than freelance for other companies, you'll need to know the business aspects of creating greeting cards. Printing and marketing your work are the major considerations when self-publishing.

Finding a Printer

This is where you judge a book (or card) by its cover. Quality printing is everything. People buy blank cards based on the artwork alone.

Offset Printing

There are different kinds of printing. If you want to reproduce your artwork in just one color (like a simple pen-and-ink drawing), then offset printing is all you need. Offset printing is inexpensive and can be done by most printers. You can find printers in your local yellow pages. Just select the card stock and ink color you want, and you're ready to go!

Four-Color Printing

If you're reproducing a multicolor watercolor painting or colored pencil drawing, you'll need to print using the four-color process. Not all printers are equipped to handle this process. Equipment and costs vary considerably, so do some comparison shopping.

The cost per card is less expensive the more cards you print. For a fair price, plan on printing 2,500 cards. You can also "gang" several card designs together on the same sheet of paper. This allows you to yield more designs per printing job and save some money. This is especially beneficial to do when you are just starting out and don't know what cards will sell best.

Mail-Order Printers

Artists' magazines and trade publications have ads for some of the large printers that operate by mail. This may not always be a good value, but it is worth checking into.

I've used one of the large printers that works by mail and was very happy with the results. However, this printer was more expensive on a per card cost. If your plan is to sell retail at shows, then you can make a profit using a mail-order printer. But if you want to sell wholesale, you may not have a good enough profit margin using this printing method.

Small-Run Printing

A short run of printing can be done on a color laser copier. The quality of these machines has improved over the last few years and yields good quality prints. Also, improvements to computer printers, and scanners has made it possible for the do-it-yourselfer to publish right at home.

PAPER STOCK

Take stock of paper stock. Visit a good paper supplier to find what you want. There are many different weights, colors, textures and finishes. Some printers can show you their stock; however, it's usually less expensive to buy the stock directly from the paper supplier. Be sure your printer's equipment can handle the card stock you select.

Pricing and Packaging Self-Published Cards

If you are just starting out and have little capital to invest, self-marketing is the way to start. Many artists who participate in outdoor arts and crafts shows sell their framed art along with their cards, and some even mat or frame their cards. If you sell directly to the customer, you can eliminate the middleman and make more money for yourself.

Pricing

SINGLE CARDS

To price your own cards, look at what other artists charge for a similar product and check the prices in stores. This will help you set your price. In the 1990s, single cards from $.75 to $2.50 each are fairly priced. If you're selling hand-painted, one-of-a-kind cards, $3.50 to $7.50 is the average price range. A formula for pricing based on a per card cost basis is explained at right.

BOXED CARDS

The price of your boxed cards should be in line with other artists' cards and cards sold in stores. You'll make less money per card, but you'll sell more in volume. A box of eight cards and envelopes currently retails for $2.50 to $12 on an average. Unique handmade cards usually are not sold in boxes.

Packaging

SETS OF CARDS

If you plan to sell your cards in sets, whether in bags or boxes, eight cards and envelopes is the average count. Some artists have sets of six or ten. If you are selling holiday cards, sets of twelve, fifteen, eighteen, twenty or twenty-five are the typical counts per bag or box.

BAGS OR BOXES?

When I first started out, I bagged my cards in clear plastic, which cost me approximately 25 percent less than boxes. However, when I began to box my cards, my sales doubled every year thereafter.

BOX MANUFACTURERS

Box manufacturers can be found in your local yellow pages or in giftware trade publications. The boxes are a more professional way to present your product and give you a competitive edge at arts and crafts shows.

PRICE CHART

Planning a price for your cards can be figured on a per card cost basis. This is a guide, not a rule.

1. Take the cost of making one card, including the cost of the envelope.
2. Double that amount (this will be your wholesale price).
3. The retailer will double the wholesale cost.

If the retail price is a marketable price, then you have a good plan. If the price is too high, then you are paying too much for printing.

Direct Mail

Another way to sell your cards is by direct mail. Whether you use the post office or E-mail, you need to develop a sales tool. The best sales tool is a color catalog.

Catalogs

You can find printers for your catalog just like you would for your cards—through trade publications and your local yellow pages. Do a bit of shopping around to find out competitive prices. There's a wide range of costs involved with the four-color method of producing a catalog.

An important word of advice: Do not put prices in your catalog. It's more cost-effective to have at least two thousand catalogs printed. If your prices change during the year or from year to year, your catalog will be outdated before you even begin selling. Do not print the date on the catalog either for the same reason. Instead provide a price sheet insert using a separate black-and-white page that you can photocopy inexpensively in smaller quantities.

Before you print your catalog, you need to decide if you are selling wholesale (to stores) or retail (to the consumer), or if you will do both. The black-and-white pricing sheet inserted in your catalog can be customized to accommodate your market.

Mailing List for Your Catalog

Use your local yellow pages to develop a mailing list. You can also buy mailing lists (check the yellow pages and trade publications). A good library will have a CD-ROM for American businesses. You can print the addresses of gift and card stores from all over the U.S., or just your state or local area.

Door-to-Door

You can self-market your cards to stores using the door-to-door method. This entails developing a "road" plan. Find the names, addresses and phone numbers of likely stores, and call them to set up appointments. You'll find that many small stores like to buy directly from the artist. Only you can know all about your product and do the best job of presenting and selling it.

Make Friends

Plan as many stops in one day as you can. If you average one hour per store, figure on visiting six to eight stores. Make the most of your road time. The fun part of marketing in this way is making new friends. Often you can get leads for other prospective clients by asking the store's buyer if he knows of any other stores, shows and so on that might be interested in your cards.

Most store owners go to trade shows and are willing to share what they know. Ask them for information about the shows that they attend, and plan to attend some yourself.

While you are on the road, you may pass a newly opened store. If you have time, stop and introduce yourself. Most buyers want to work by appointment, but if it is a slow day, they may see you.

Always have your catalog on hand to leave with the buyers. If they can't see or buy from you that day, at least they can look over your catalog when convenient. Be sure to make a follow-up call for an order.

Sales Representatives

If your plan is to market to a larger territory, you may want to consider working with an independent sales representative. Sales reps cover more mileage and can represent you in areas that you wouldn't be able to cover yourself—like across the country.

Working with a local sales rep is also good. The time that you spend on the road selling keeps you from doing more artwork. The artists who market their own cards usually spend 90 percent of their time on business and 10 percent of their time creating the art. Only you can decide how you want to spend your time.

You will need to provide your rep with a deck of your cards. (A deck is a sample of each one of your cards.) If you box your cards, provide the rep with a sample of one box. Many reps will not need a copy of your catalog, but they will need a price sheet.

Another advantage of having a sales rep is that they usually go to trade shows. There are many small local shows, and major shows are held in the big cities. Sales reps usually expect you to pay a percentage of their booth fee. You may also need to supply them with more catalogs and decks. Many reps write sales at these shows, so this would be a good investment for you. Be sure to ask how much space they are giving you for the cost. A friend of mine paid a few hundred dollars for the New York Gift Show and only got one square foot of space for his product!

Fees

Sales reps are paid the industry standard of 15 to 20 percent commission of the wholesale price, and they are paid once a month.

Finding a Sales Representative

There are some very good and very bad reps out there. Unfortunately, there's no way to tell how to find a good one. If they love your product, chances are they will do well selling it. And if it sells easily, they will show it.

Finding an independent sales rep can be done in a few ways. My best reps were found by word of mouth. A store may recommend someone. Some reps know other reps. The trade publications advertise lists of reps. Some reps take out their own ads for their territory. You can also place your own ad asking for reps for a certain territory. Some reps have small territories and numbers of clients and work out of their homes; others have larger territories and numbers of clients and have showrooms. (Avoid reps that want money up front unless it is for a trade show.) Check their references. Ask them questions. Find out how long they have been in business. Do they work full or part time? What other products do they represent? What kinds of stores do they call on? Do they collect money that is past due?

Gallery

Valerie Falso creates watercolor paintings, makes cards of her art and sells them at arts and crafts shows.

SUMMER FRUIT
Valerie Falso

LACE
Valerie Falso

SNOW SCENE—CHRISTMAS
Pauline Monz

Pauline Monz sells her hand-painted, one-of-a-kind cards in a local shop.

STARS OF
SPRING
© *Susan Spencer*

Susan Spencer is a
nationally known
artist who sells her
cards at arts and
crafts shows.

ARTS BY ASHLEY
Sarah Ashley Blakeley

Sarah Ashley Blakeley self-publishes her cards
and sells them via catalogs, trade shows and
sales representatives.

GARDENS
Deborah W. Rogers

"Gardens"   Deborah W Rogers 97"

Deborah Rogers paints unique cards on premade card stock and sells them in galleries and at art shows.

TULIPS
Deborah W. Rogers

"Tulips"   Deborah W Rogers 98

SKATING ON CAZENOVIA LAKE
©Linda E. Doust

Linda Doust paints whimsical scenes of villages.

THANK-YOU
©NRN Designs
Design by Navina Capecci

PANSY
©Cape Shore, Inc.
From an original design by Kristin Stashenko

SEASIDE WREATH
©Cape Shore, Inc.
From an original design by Jeanette Robertson

WAITING FOR NEXT TIME
© Cape Shore, Inc.
From an original design by Jeanette Robertson

BLACK-AND-WHITE COWS
© Notations
From an original design by Jeanette Robertson

Index